NEW ZEALAND

EXTINCT SPECIES

HUIA

JENNY JONES

Heinemann
PRIMARY

Jenny Jones wishes to express her thanks and gratitude to Trevor Worthy for his expertise and comments.

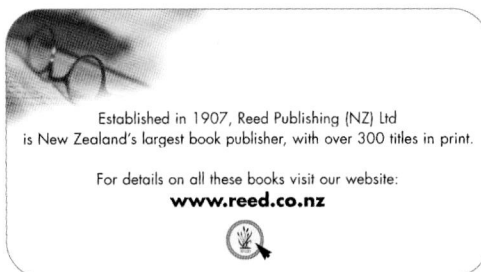

Established in 1907, Reed Publishing (NZ) Ltd is New Zealand's largest book publisher, with over 300 titles in print.
For details on all these books visit our website:
www.reed.co.nz

Published by Heinemann Education, a division of Reed Publishing (NZ) Ltd,
39 Rawene Rd, Birkenhead, Auckland.
Associated companies, branches and representatives throughout the world.

ISBN 1 86944 452 3
© 2001 Jenny Jones
The author asserts her moral rights in the work.

Picture credits
Alexander Turnbull Library: 7 (top), 14
Department of Conservation: 4 (both), 10–11, 12, 18 (both)
Dave Gunson: 8, 9, 17, 21
Jenny Jones: 6, 19, 20, 23
Rod Morris: cover, 1, 3, 5, 13, 15, 22
Jeanette Winn: 7 (bottom)

Book design by Nicole Merrie

First published 2001

Printed in New Zealand by Brebner Print Ltd

CONTENTS

THE SPECIES

Until quite recently, the huia lived in the safety of New Zealand's North Island forests. The ancestors of the huia are thought to have lived in New Zealand for about 65 million years.

Huia were wattlebirds. There were three species of wattlebirds found in New Zealand — the kokako, the saddleback and the huia.

The kokako, with its haunting song, is now a threatened species. The saddleback, with its dark cinnamon-coloured back or saddle, is also a threatened species, and is only found on small offshore islands. The huia is extinct.

The huia was a large, forest-dwelling bird. Males and females were about the same size — approximately the size of a magpie. It was also the largest of our three wattlebird species.

North Island kokako

North Island saddleback

Huia

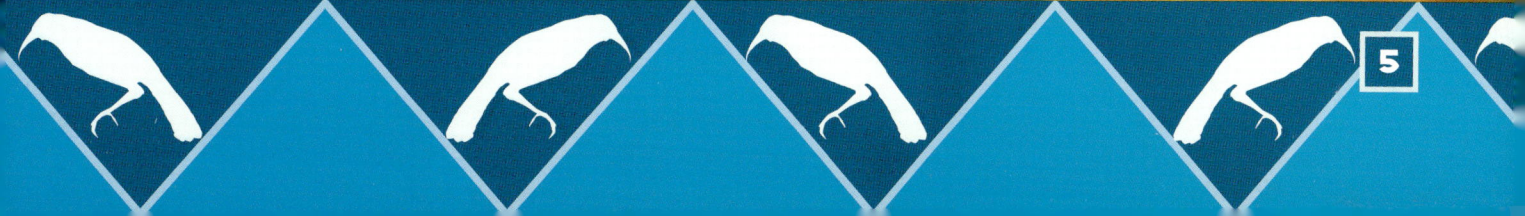

APPEARANCE

The huia was without doubt one of the most beautiful birds found in the New Zealand forest.

The plumage of the adult male and female huia was almost identical. The feathers were glossy black with shiny green on the upper surfaces, especially the head.

The twelve tail feathers were very unusual. They had a 2 cm band of pure white across the tips. No other bird in New Zealand had white-tipped tail feathers like this. When they flew, the tail feathers spread open just like a fan.

At the base and on each side of the beak were bright-orange fleshy wattles. The wattles were actually extensions of the lining of the mouth. Why these birds had wattles is not clear. It is thought the wattles were used in mating displays.

It was very easy to tell the male from the female by their beaks. Both were a whitish-cream, but the shapes were very different. The male huia had a stout and slightly arched bill of about 6 cm in length. The female had a more slender and strongly curved bill that was about 8–10 cm long.

Their legs were a dark bluish-grey and they had large claws.

Huia had a strong tail and it was used as a prop when they were gripping onto branches while feeding or resting.

EATING HABITS

Huia were diurnal (daytime feeders) and hunted for their food in the undergrowth and on the ground. The huia never left the shade of the forest which it shared with other birds like piopio, saddlebacks, parakeets, fantails, wrens, riflemen, kokako, hihi and kereru.

The huia ate invertebrates, feeding on large insects and, in particular, the larvae of wood-boring beetles and adult beetles. A pair of huia would normally feed together, but did not appear to help each other in the search for food.

When feeding, the male gripped the tree trunk like a woodpecker does, with his legs forward and tail pushed hard onto the trunk. In this position he could tear off rotting wood with his strong beak to get at the beetles and huhu-grub larvae.

The female could probe her much longer beak deep down into the decaying wood to reach huhu and other beetles. She would pull them out, hold them down with her foot and tear off the hard parts. The insects would then be picked up, turned lengthwise in the beak and swallowed whole.

It was easy to see where huia had been feeding in the decayed wood of big old forest trees. Other food consisted of fruits of the hinau, pigeonwood, pokaka and karamu. While feeding, the huia uttered a soft whistle.

HABITAT

Fossil bones of the huia have only been found in the North Island. The dense forests of rimu, rata, kahikatea and beech trees had thick undergrowth which provided the habitat huia preferred. Typical huia habitat was found in the Kaimanawa, Ruahine, Tararua and Rimutaka ranges. It was here that the last small numbers of huia were seen until 1907.

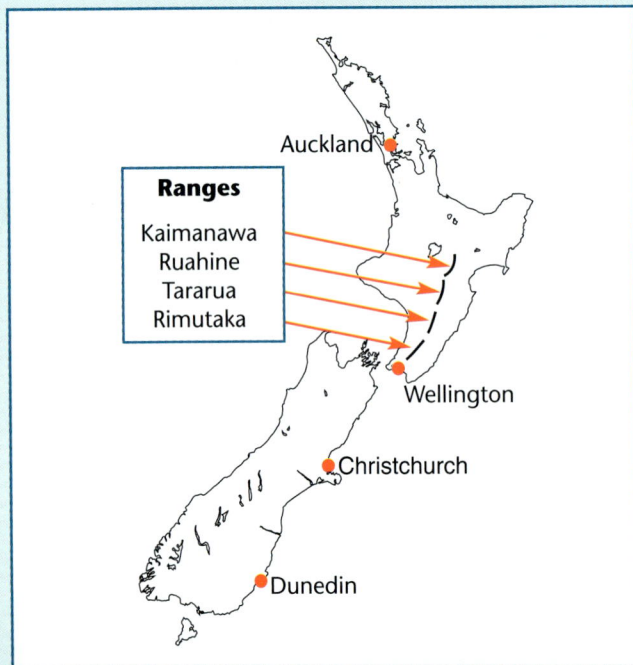

Ranges

Kaimanawa
Ruahine
Tararua
Rimutaka

Auckland

Wellington

Christchurch

Dunedin

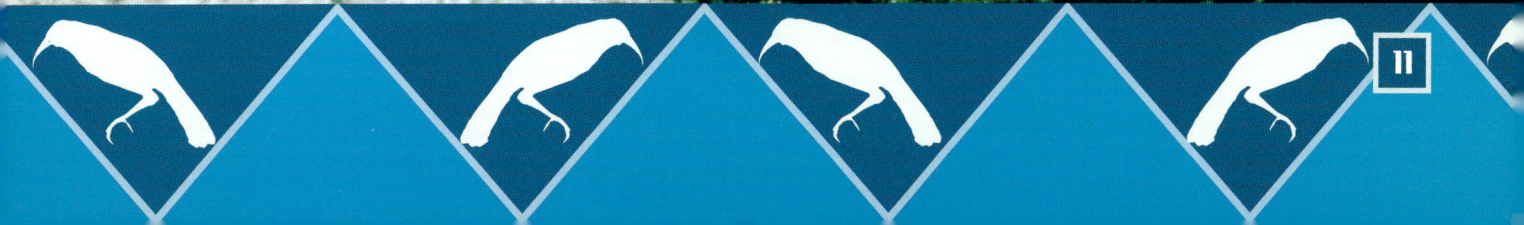

PREDATORS

The huia's natural predators were the laughing owl, the Eyles' harrier (both now extinct), the Australasian harrier and the falcon, which are still seen today.

The laughing owl was a nocturnal hunter and would have taken huia at dusk. Both the harriers and the falcon were diurnal (daytime hunters).

They would have used their powerful eyesight to prey on huia as they moved about in trees.

Maori were the first human hunters of huia, followed by Europeans. Both thought the beaks and tail feathers were beautiful and valuable.

Australasian harrier

Laughing owl

BREEDING

The male and female huia appeared to bond for life. They were often seen in pairs and would constantly call to each other. They became very distressed if they lost their mate. At night the pair would roost on a branch huddled together.

The breeding season was in early summer (October to November). Huia nested on or near the ground, usually at the foot of an old tree where they were sheltered by overhanging plants. They built large nests from sticks and astelia leaves. The nest was about 36 cm across, with a small cup about 18 cm wide and 5 cm deep in the middle. The cup was lined with soft materials like mosses and feathers to protect and insulate the eggs and chicks.

The female laid 2–4 grey eggs that were much smaller than a chicken egg, with dark purple, grey and brown spots. The huia carried the eggshell well away from the nest site once the young hatched. This may have been to hide the location of the young.

The female got very fat before the breeding season and, while she was on the nest, the male fed her. She lost the feathers from her chest and belly during the breeding season.

Huia nest and egg

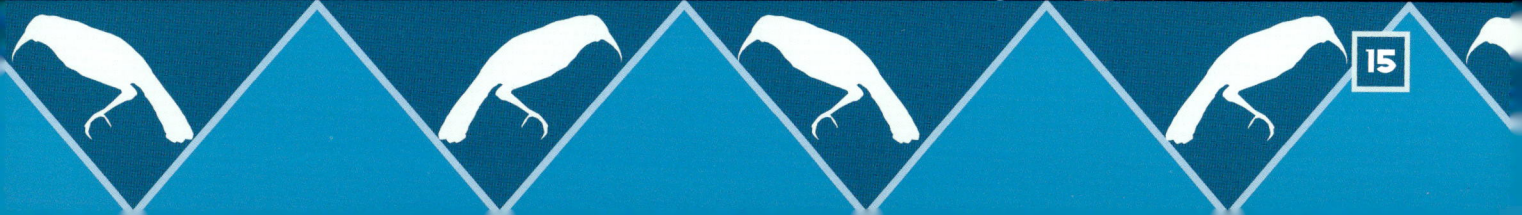

YOUNG

The young hatched in November. They were fed by their parents for some time after they fledged (left the nest). At this age, they were as big as their parents, but their parents were kept busy supplying the chicks with food such as huhu grubs, insects and spiders.

Young huia had a distinctive, low, sorrowful cry that was easily recognised.

Their beaks looked similar when they were young, but changed as they became adults.

It is thought that the huia was similar to the kokako, another wattlebird, and did not breed every year.

The feathers of the juvenile huia had brown spread throughout. The feathers of young females were duller than young males. The tail feathers were tipped with white, like an adult, but they had reddish-brown and yellow colours as well. The wattles of the juvenile huia were a fleshy-white.

The huia was very trusting. There are reports that the female allowed herself to be handled by humans while on the nest.

CAUSES OF EXTINCTION

Huia feathers were considered to be very beautiful and valuable by early Maori and were used for decoration and trading. You can read more about this in the fact-file section on page 22.

When Europeans arrived in New Zealand, they too thought the feathers of the huia were beautiful and they became worth a lot of money to collectors. Many of the trusting huia were shot and exhibited in museums both in New Zealand and Great Britain. Humans were the major cause of the extinction of the huia.

Ferret

Stoat

Habitat destruction and the introduction of ferrets, stoats and weasels also contributed to the extinction of the huia. These animals were introduced to control rabbit populations, but they found the huia and their eggs and chicks much easier prey. Huia could not adapt to life in regenerating forests, as they needed the old unchanging forests.

By the early part of last century, soon after 1907, the huia is thought to have become extinct.

FOSSILS TELL A STORY

Fossilised huia bones tell scientists that huia were quite widespread. They have been found as far north as North Cape, and in major fossil localities at several sites near Gisborne, and at Waitomo and Puketitiri. Fossil bones of this bird are rare, however.

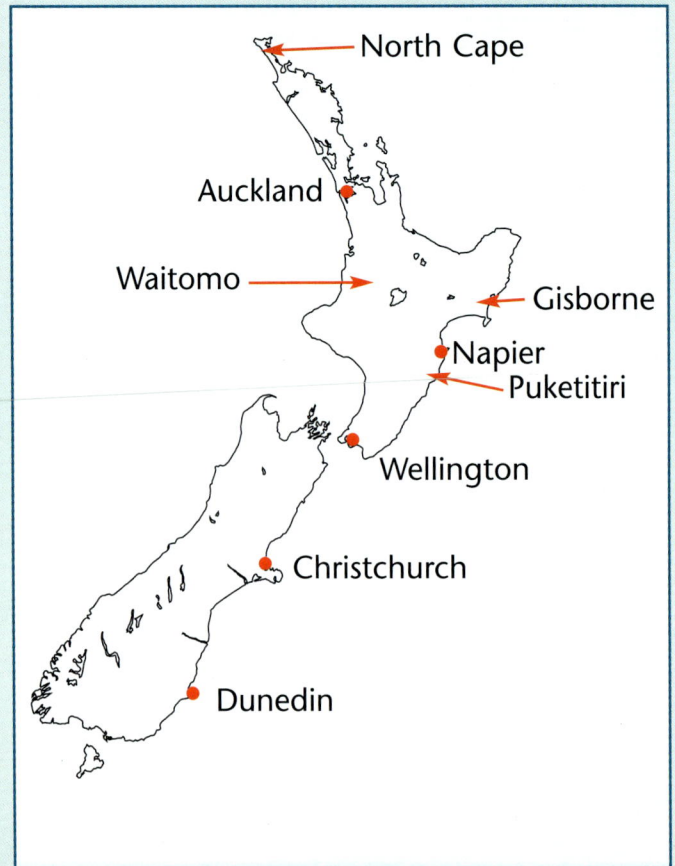

FACT FILE

Behaviour

Huia moved along on the ground very quickly by hopping. The male usually led the female. Huia pairs were playful birds and were often preening each other's feathers and making low calls to each other. They were never still for very long, constantly spreading their tail into a broad fan.

Huia moved quickly up and down through the forest trees, spreading out their tail feathers and throwing up their wings as they jumped along the ground or from tree to tree, much like the kokako still does today. They were generally seen in pairs or in a party of four or more.

The huia had an unusual resting position. It held its beak high up in the air with one leg holding onto an upper branch and the other leg downwards. The tail was up, giving the bird an outward curving back.

Tail feathers

The tail feathers were very significant and prized by early Maori. They were often used in trade with other tribes where the huia was not found. They were a taonga and kept safe in a waka huia, an ornately carved box. Maori of high rank used the feathers as adornments. The beak and skin were also used as adornments. Early Maori found that imitating the huia's call soon brought this trusting bird close enough to capture.

Waka huia

Song

The huia got its name from the shrill whistle repeated over and over, which was its alarm cry. This call from a huia always attracted other huia.

The huia had a range of calls: a soft clear whistle of long and short notes which they repeated, a high-pitched whistling note when alarmed or excited and low chuckling notes that sometimes sounded like a puppy whining. Some of the songs of huia were very much like those of the kokako, only softer. To hear both kokako and huia singing together would have been beautiful.

Huia were special. It is a real loss that they were not considered worth more alive than dead. Because of their unusual appearance, their beautiful song, their trusting nature, and their inability to withstand predators, they are lost for all time.

Huia with kokako

INDEX